EARTH BY NUMBERS

Habitats and Biomes

Nancy Dickmann

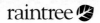

raintree
a Capstone company — publishers for children

Raintree is an imprint of Capstone Global Library Limited, a company incorporated in England and Wales having its registered office at 264 Banbury Road, Oxford, OX2 7DY – Registered company number: 6695582

www.raintree.co.uk
myorders@raintree.co.uk

Text © Capstone Global Library Limited 2019
The moral rights of the proprietor have been asserted.

Produced for Raintree by Calcium
Editors: Sarah Eason and Harriet McGregor
Designer: Paul Myerscough
Originated by Capstone Global Library Limited © 2018
Printed and bound in India

ISBN 978 1 4747 6539 8 (hardback)
22 21 20 19 18
10 9 8 7 6 5 4 3 2 1

ISBN 978 1 4747 6545 9 (paperback)
23 22 21 20 19
10 9 8 7 6 5 4 3 2 1

British Library Cataloguing in Publication Data
A full catalogue record for this book is available from the British Library.

Acknowledgements
Picture credits: Cover: Shutterstock: Apichart Sripa; Insides: Shutterstock: Barbara Barbour 16, Bikeriderlondon 15, Bartosz Budrewicz 6, Cvalle 25, F9photos 8–9, Alex Frank 4–5, Arina P Habich 26–27, Jorg Hackemann 1, 22–23, Holbox 9, Lorraine Hudgins 22, Kletr 21, 28–29, Serguei Koultchitskii 5, Lenar Musin 12, Neelsky 28, Carlos Neto 20–21, Bill Perry 24, Catalin Petolea 6–7, Ricardo Reitmeyer 27, Nicram Sabod 14–15, Seb2583 19, Heather Lucia Snow 11, Popova Valeriya 10, Anke van Wyk 12–13, Vlad61 18–19, Tom Willard 16–17.

Every effort has been made to contact copyright holders of material reproduced in this book. Any omissions will be rectified in subsequent printings if notice is given to the publisher.

All the internet addresses (URLs) given in this book were valid at the time of going to press. However, due to the dynamic nature of the internet, some addresses may have changed, or sites may have changed or ceased to exist since publication. While the author and publisher regret any inconvenience this may cause readers, no responsibility for any such changes can be accepted by either the author or the publisher.

Contents

Some words are shown in bold, **like this**. You can find out what they mean by looking in the glossary.

What is a biome?

Every living thing lives in a **biome**. A biome is a geographic area that has different weather, landforms and plant life from other regions. For example, **deserts** are usually considered to be a biome, and so are forests and oceans.

Within each biome you can find many different **ecosystems**. An ecosystem is not just a place; it is a system made up of the plants, animals and non-living things in a particular area. They depend on each other to survive. An ecosystem can be as small as a pond or a rotting log that is home to fungi, insects and other small animals.

For an animal or plant to survive, it must have a **habitat** that provides everything it needs. Its habitat must have food and water, and there must be shelter to protect the **organism** from **predators** and weather.

EARTH BY NUMBERS

Over many generations, animal and plant species slowly change to become better suited to their habitat. If one organism has a **trait** that helps it to survive, it will pass this trait on to its offspring. Because of the helpful trait, they will be more likely to survive to pass the trait on to their own offspring. This is called **adaptation**.

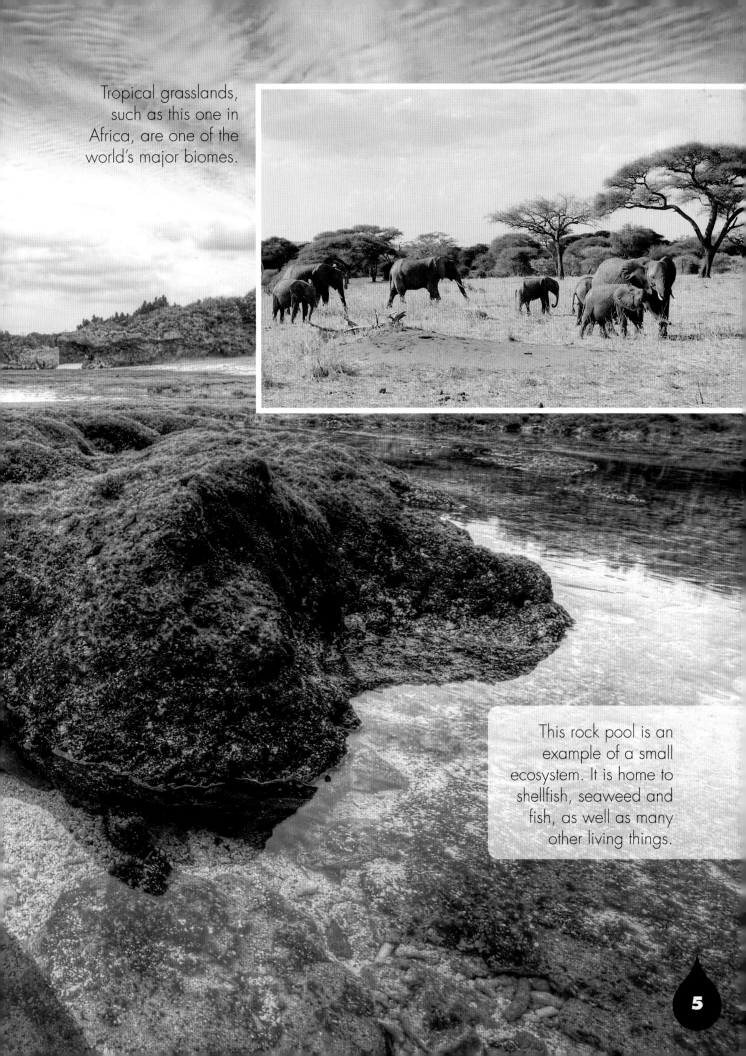

Tropical grasslands, such as this one in Africa, are one of the world's major biomes.

This rock pool is an example of a small ecosystem. It is home to shellfish, seaweed and fish, as well as many other living things.

Deciduous forests

Deciduous forests are areas of trees that lose their leaves in winter. These forests are contain many other types of smaller plants, as well as a lot of different animals. The forests cover large areas of Europe and North America, as well as parts of Asia and Australia.

Deer, wolves, bears and other large animals make their homes in deciduous forests. Many smaller animals, such as badgers, foxes, mice and birds, are also found there. The leaf litter on the forest floor makes a perfect home for many different insects and other invertebrates.

In the winter, the habitat changes as the trees' leaves die and fall to the ground. This helps the forest, because the rotting leaves keep the soil rich. But in the winter, there is less food to eat. Many animals that live in the forests survive the winter by **hibernating**.

Hedgehogs hibernate in winter, between November and March, in nests made of piles of leaves.

A different type of forest is found to the north of the world's deciduous forests. These forests are made up of trees called conifers, which have needle-like leaves that do not fall off in winter. Winters are long and harsh, but the trees are adapted to this **climate**.

Rotting logs such as this one provide a perfect home for some types of insects, as well as mosses, ferns and fungi.

Rainforests

Tropical rainforests are one of Earth's most amazing biomes, because they are home to so many different plants and animals. Found in hot, humid places, these forests have the same conditions all year round.

In a tropical rainforest, the tops of the trees form a thick layer called the canopy. It is so thick that very little light gets through to the forest floor. The plants that live below the canopy have adapted to survive with little light.

Many rainforest animals live in the trees, including birds, monkeys, snakes, bats and insects. They fly, glide or swing from branch to branch. Larger animals, such as gorillas, anteaters and leopards, live on the forest floor, along with smaller animals such as rodents and insects. The dappled light there helps them to hide from predators or sneak up on prey.

EARTH BY NUMBERS

Rainforests are also found in cooler places, such as the northern part of the west coast of the United States. These **temperate** rainforests get a lot of rain, and they are often home to big coniferous trees. Mosses and **lichens** also do well in this damp environment.

Tropical rainforests cover only 6 per cent of Earth's surface, but they contain more than 50 per cent of the world's plant and animal species.

These spider monkeys' feet and hands are adapted for grasping trees. They can also use their tails as an extra limb.

FOREST BIOMES—BY NUMBERS!

Forests cover **31** per cent of Earth's land surface, taking up nearly 40.4 million square kilometres (15.6 million sq miles). This area is constantly getting smaller, however, and each year about 51,800 square kilometres (20,000 sq miles) are lost.

The world's biggest rainforest is the Amazon in South America. It covers an area of

5.9 million

square kilometres (2.3 million sq miles). But the boreal forest in Russia, made up of conifer trees, is even bigger. It covers 12 million sq km (4.6 million sq miles) and contains more than 55 per cent of the world's conifers.

The tallest living thing in the world is a tree: a coast redwood in California, USA, that measures over

metres (375 feet) tall.

California is also home to one of the world's oldest living things. A bristlecone pine tree called Methuselah is more than

4,800

years old.

Scientists believe that the Amazon rainforest is home to several million species of animals and plants. It has more types of animals and plants than anywhere else on Earth.

Deserts

Rainforests make a perfect habitat for some plants and animals, but living things can also survive in much drier biomes. Deserts are areas that have very little rain – sometimes it can be many years between one storm and the next! We often think of deserts as hot and sandy, but many deserts are rocky, and some are cold. In fact, the world's largest desert is in Antarctica. It is covered in water, mostly in the form of ice, but very little new snow falls there.

Surviving in a desert is hard, but some plants and animals have adapted to make use of the small amounts of water that are found there. For example, a cactus has a lot of roots for soaking up water. Its thick, fleshy stem can swell to store large amounts of water until it is needed. Cacti have another advantage – they don't have leaves, so they can't lose water through them as other plants do.

Camels are perfectly adapted to live in the desert. They can cope with high temperatures and can go for a long time without drinking.

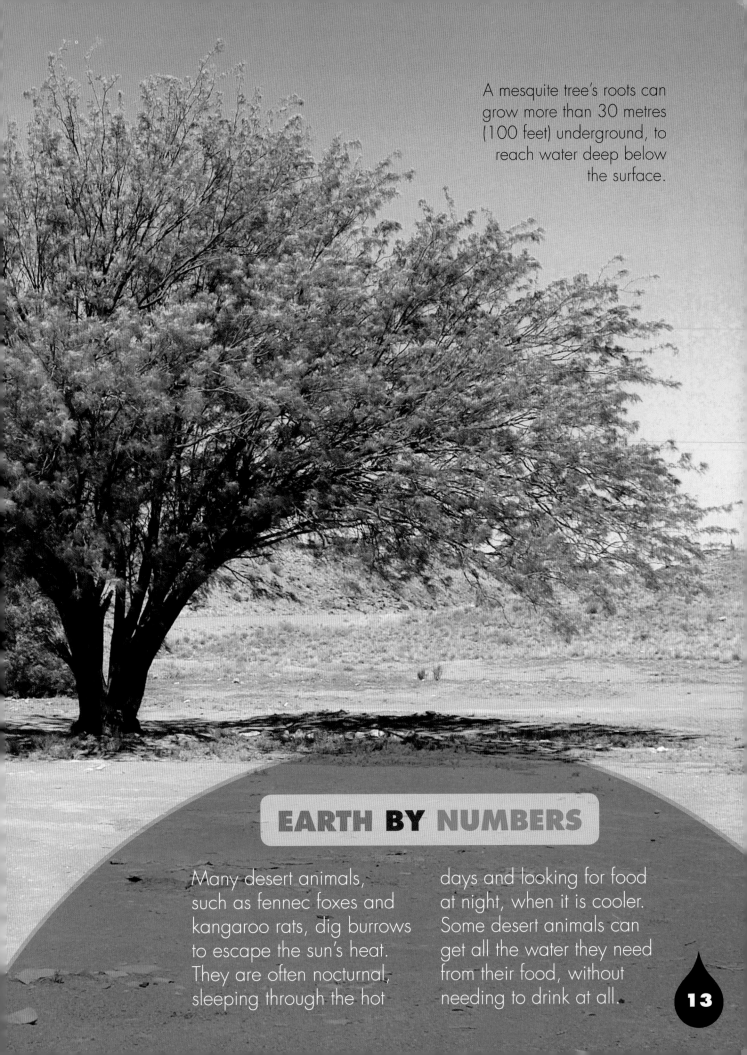

A mesquite tree's roots can grow more than 30 metres (100 feet) underground, to reach water deep below the surface.

EARTH BY NUMBERS

Many desert animals, such as fennec foxes and kangaroo rats, dig burrows to escape the sun's heat. They are often nocturnal, sleeping through the hot days and looking for food at night, when it is cooler. Some desert animals can get all the water they need from their food, without needing to drink at all.

Tundra

Another example of an extreme habitat is cold, windy tundra. Tundra is treeless places that are found in the far north of the planet. There are also some tundra zones on the tops of mountains. The tundra has long winters and very short summers, and very little rain.

Tundra soil is poor, and below the surface it is permanently frozen. Roots cannot push through the **permafrost**, so it is mostly smaller plants that grow in tundra soil. Being short helps the plants cope with strong winds. Small shrubs, grasses and mosses are common tundra plants. Wildflowers often bloom during the short summers.

Animals that live in the tundra are adapted to the cold climate. Many have thick layers of fur and fat to keep them warm. Some tundra animals, such as Arctic ground squirrels, hibernate during the winter. Others animals, such as snow buntings and other birds, **migrate** south to warmer areas.

EARTH BY NUMBERS

Some tundra animals can look very different, depending on the season. The Arctic fox, snowshoe hare and stoat are all brown in the summer, but their fur turns white in the winter. This makes them harder to spot against the snow, which can help them hide from predators or sneak up on prey.

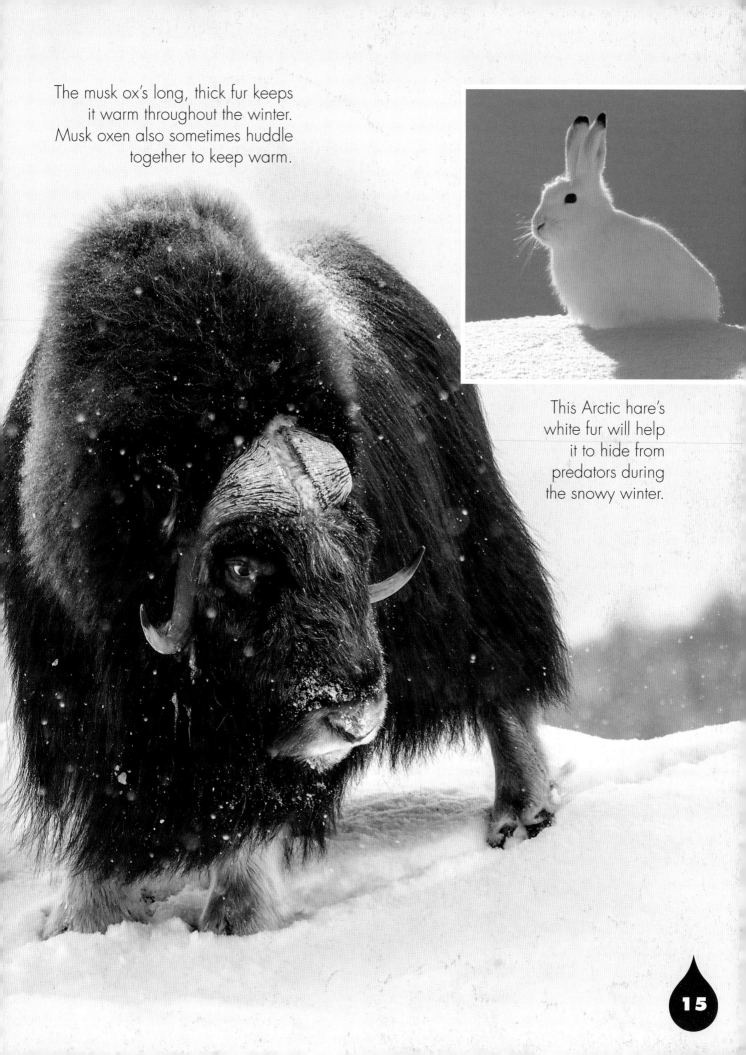

The musk ox's long, thick fur keeps it warm throughout the winter. Musk oxen also sometimes huddle together to keep warm.

This Arctic hare's white fur will help it to hide from predators during the snowy winter.

EXTREME HABITATS—BY NUMBERS!

The average winter temperature in the tundra is

-34° Celsius

(−30° Fahrenheit). It only rises above freezing during the short summers, when it averages 3–12° Celsius (37–54° Fahrenheit).

In some hot deserts, such as the Sahara in Africa, temperatures can reach as high as

54° Celsius

(130° F) during the day, though it is much colder at night. The temperature in the colder Gobi Desert in China can go up or down by as much as 16° C (60° F) in just 24 hours!

Deserts get no more than

25 centimetres (10 inches)

of **precipitation** per year. Although its surface is dotted with bogs and ponds, the Arctic tundra gets only 15–25 cm (6–10 inches) of precipitation per year (which includes melting snow).

The saguaro cactus swells up after a rainfall, and about

90

per cent of its body can be used to store water. A single cactus can hold 1 tonne of water.

Humans can live for between three and five days without water. Some camels have been known to survive for six or seven months without water, but in the hottest summer months they can last only about five days without a drink. A camel can drink

114

litres (30 gallons) of water in just 13 minutes!

Oceans

Oceans are the biggest biome on Earth, covering about 71 per cent of the planet's surface. The deeper you go, the darker and colder the ocean gets. The **pressure** of the water above becomes enormous, too. Without special equipment, humans can only survive in the top layers of the oceans.

Scientists divide the oceans into layers. The sunlight zone is at the top. Here, there is enough sunlight for plants, such as kelp and algae, to make food and survive. Many fish, shellfish, star fish and other invertebrates live here, as well as mammals such as whales and dolphins.

Below the sunlight zone is the twilight zone, where there is very little light. Even deeper is the midnight zone, where there is no light at all. Many of the animals that live here are soft-bodied, so they can absorb the immense water pressure without being crushed.

Coral reefs are found in the sunlight zone. They provide a habitat for many different fish and other sea creatures.

EARTH BY NUMBERS

When the tide goes out, it can leave pools of seawater among the rocks and sand. These tidal pools are home to creatures such as shellfish, sea anemones and seaweed. When the tide comes in and goes out, it brings new organisms and allows others to escape back into the ocean.

Most sea animals can get oxygen from the water, but mammals such as whales and dolphins must come to the surface to breathe.

Freshwater biomes

Earth's rivers, ponds and lakes hold only a small amount of water compared to the oceans. But they are still important habitats. The animals and plants that live in these freshwater habitats don't need the adaptations that allow sea creatures to live in salt water.

Rivers, lakes and ponds are home to plants such as algae. Animals that live there range from insects and fish to larger animals such as crocodiles. As well as the animals that live in the water, these freshwater habitats provide drinking water for land animals.

The water in lakes and ponds is still, but plants and animals that live in rivers must adapt to flowing water. Some attach themselves to the riverbed with roots or suckers. Fish called darters have a long, thin, streamlined shape that makes it easier to swim against the current (flow of water). Other fish have fins that help them to hold on to rocks.

EARTH BY NUMBERS

A few animals can live in either fresh or salt water. For example, salmon lay their eggs in fresh water. The baby salmon stay there for up to four years before travelling to the oceans to find food. After several years at sea, they return to the river where they were born, to reproduce.

Plants such as papyrus use their roots to hold themselves in place in the water.

Catfish often live in murky water, so they use their whisker-like barbels and sense of smell to find food.

21

Wetlands

Some habitats are a mix of water and land. These wetlands exist all over the world, wherever the land is **saturated** with water. This means that the soil has so much water in it that it cannot soak up any more. Some wetlands are completely covered by water for part of the year. Swamps, marshes and bogs are all types of wetlands.

Some trees that grow in wetlands have adaptations that allow them to live partly underwater. For example, a mangrove tree's tall, stilt-like roots help hold its trunk and branches out of the water. The roots also provide shelter for crabs and other animals, while the branches hold birds' nests.

Many different reptiles and amphibians are found in wetlands, including frogs, toads, turtles, snakes and alligators. These animals have adapted to cope with the wetlands' changing water levels.

Wetlands are home to wading birds such as herons. They walk through the water on their long legs, looking for food.

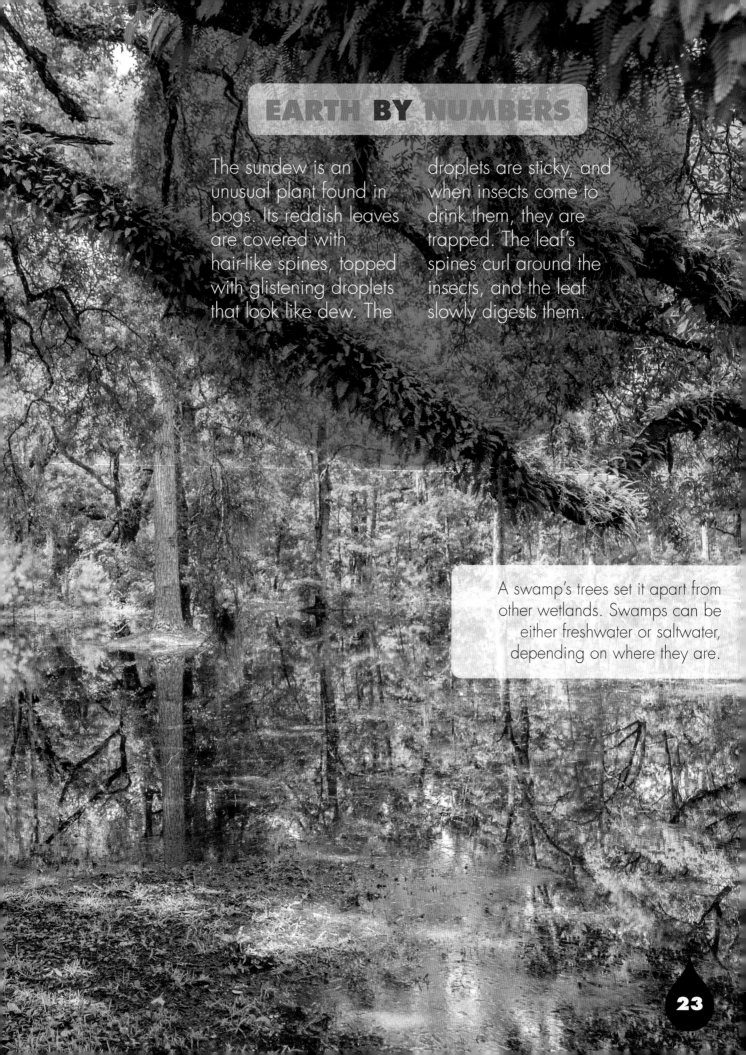

The sundew is an unusual plant found in bogs. Its reddish leaves are covered with hair-like spines, topped with glistening droplets that look like dew. The droplets are sticky, and when insects come to drink them, they are trapped. The leaf's spines curl around the insects, and the leaf slowly digests them.

A swamp's trees set it apart from other wetlands. Swamps can be either freshwater or saltwater, depending on where they are.

LIVING IN WATER—BY NUMBERS!

More than **96** per cent of Earth's water is found in the oceans. Only 2.5 per cent is fresh water, and of this tiny amount, only 1.2 per cent is liquid water that is found on Earth's surface. The rest of it is found underground, or frozen solid in **glaciers** and ice caps.

In 2014, scientists discovered a snailfish living in the oceans at a depth of **8,145** metres (26,722 feet). It is the deepest fish ever found.

Only **5** per cent of the salmon that make it back to the oceans after spawning survive to return and spawn a second time.

In the sunlight zone, the water temperature can range from −2 to 36° Celsius (28–97° F), depending on the location. In the midnight zone it stays constant at

4° Celsius (39° F).

Wetlands are often drained to create land for farming or houses. In the 1600s, the area that is now the United States had about 890,300 square kilometres (343,750 sq miles) of wetlands. About

50 per cent of that area remains today.

The largest protected wetland in the world is Llanos de Moxos in Bolivia. It covers more than

68,790

square kilometres (26,562 sq miles) – that's nearly the same size as Scotland!

Grasslands

Large areas of Earth's land are quite flat and covered in grasses, with few trees. These places are called grasslands. Grasslands in temperate places, such as Europe and North America, have warm summers and cold winters. They are usually called **prairies** or steppes. In tropical climates, where it is warm all year round, they are called savannahs.

Many prairie grasses have deep roots. This allows them to soak up as much water as possible. This is important in dry climates such as on the steppes. The grasses also have big root systems, so that grazing animals do not pull up the roots. The grasses can regrow from the roots.

Grassland animals have adaptations, too. For example, there are few trees to provide cover, so many grassland animals are fast runners. Some African gazelles can reach speeds of 64 kilometres (40 miles) per hour, but the cheetah can reach 105 kilometres (65 miles) per hour when chasing them.

EARTH BY NUMBERS

Bison are the largest land mammals in North America. They live on the prairies, where they graze on the grasses. Their thick, shaggy coats keep them warm during the cold winters. During the winter, they dig up the snow with their pointed horns to reach the plants beneath.

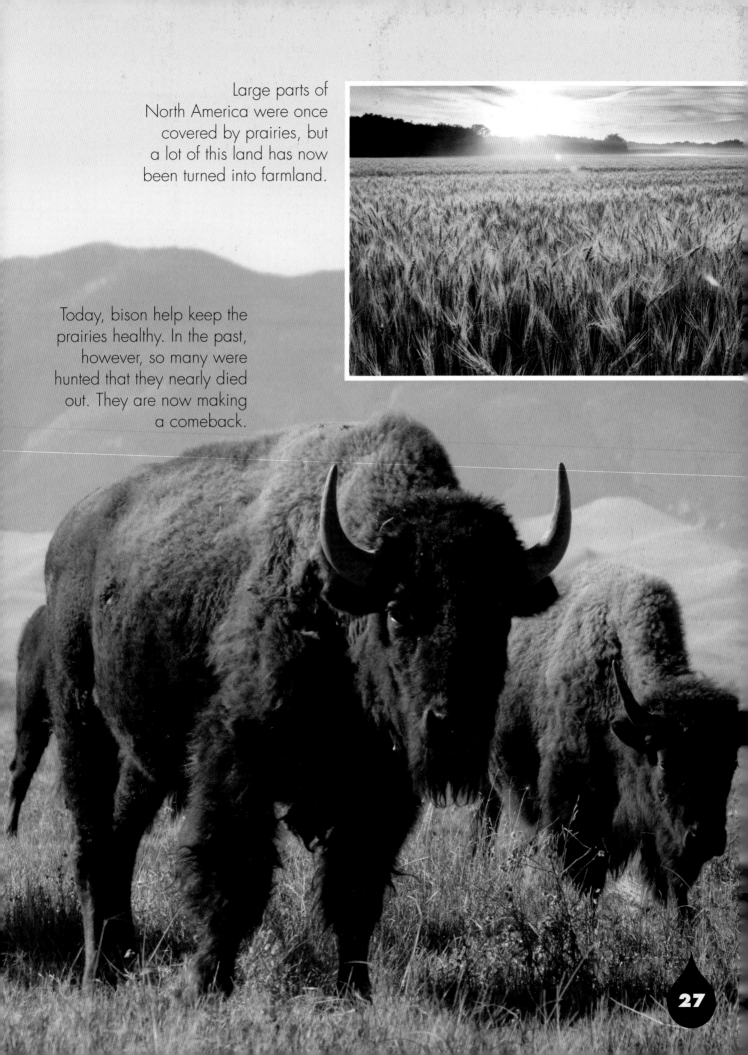

Large parts of North America were once covered by prairies, but a lot of this land has now been turned into farmland.

Today, bison help keep the prairies healthy. In the past, however, so many were hunted that they nearly died out. They are now making a comeback.

Habitats under threat

Every living thing depends on its habitat for food, water and shelter. Unfortunately, many of the most important habitats are being lost. Humans dig up prairies to plant crops, cut down forests for wood and drain wetlands to build houses. When these habitats are destroyed, the plants and animals that live there are put in danger.

Even if they are not destroyed completely, habitats can also be damaged. For example, **pollution** from factories can get into rivers, making it hard for plants and animals to survive. The **greenhouse effect** is causing water temperatures to rise, and this harms coral reefs.

Throughout Earth's history, plants and animals have adapted to survive in many different habitats. But adaptations take place over a long period of time. Most plants and animals cannot adapt quickly enough to the big changes that humans are making to their habitats. We need to work together to help protect habitats and the organisms that live there.

The tiger population has dropped by around 95 per cent in the last 100 years. Now there are only about 3,200 tigers left in the wild.

Tigers are one of the world's most endangered animals. Many of them live in jungles or forests where there are plants that the tigers can hide among as they hunt.

These habitats are being destroyed, however. The humans who live nearby also hunt the same prey as tigers, leaving less food for the tigers.

We cut down between 3 billion and 6 billion trees a year, either to use the wood or to clear the land for other uses.

Glossary

adaptation change in an organism, over time, that helps it survive and reproduce in a particular habitat

biome one of the major types of landscape, such as a desert or forest

climate usual weather conditions in a particular place

deciduous tree with leaves that die and fall off each year

deserts very dry, sandy or rocky areas with very few plants

ecosystems communities of living things, together with their environments

glaciers large masses of ice that move very slowly down slopes or across land

greenhouse effect warming of Earth's surface that takes place when heat from the Sun is trapped by gases in the atmosphere

habitat natural environment of an animal or plant

hibernating sleeping through the winter in a den or burrow to save energy

invertebrates animals without backbones inside their bodies, such as insects, crabs or squid

lichens organisms that are made up of fungus and a form of algae living together

migrate travel from one region to another to find food

organism living thing

permafrost soil below the surface that is permanently frozen

pollution process of making land, water or air dirty and not safe to use

prairies large, flat areas of land covered mainly in grasses

precipitation water that falls from the sky as rain, snow, sleet or hail

predators animals that hunt other animals for food

pressure steady pushing force upon a surface

rainforests dense woodlands with very high annual rainfall, often with trees forming a canopy

saturated not able to hold any more water

temperate having temperatures that are not too hot or cold

trait characteristic that makes a living thing different from others of the same type, for example, height or eye colour

tropical having temperatures high enough for plants to grow all year round

Find out more

Books

Deserts (Habitat Survival), Melanie Waldron (Raintree, 2013)

Earth (DKfindout!), DK (Dorling Kindersley, 2017)

Exploring Coral Reefs: A Benjamin Blog and His Inquisitive Dog Investigation (Exploring Habitats with Benjamin Blog and His Inquisitive Dog), Anita Ganeri (Raintree, 2015)

Rainforests (Explorer Travel Guides), Nick Hunter (Raintree, 2014)

Tigers (Living in the Wild: Big Cats), Anna Claybourne (Raintree, 2014)

Websites

Learn more about rainforest habitats at:
www.bbc.co.uk/guides/zxdsvcw

Find out more about wetlands and the animals who live in them at:
www.dkfindout.com/uk/animals-and-nature/habitats-and-ecosystems/wetlands

Discover more about Earth's endangered species at:
http://gowild.wwf.org.uk

Index